# The Best Damn
# GOOGLE ADWORDS
# Book

## "Maximize your results to maximize your advertising dollars"

## By
## Harry J. Misner
## www.HarryMisner.com
## "Revised Edition"

The Best Damn
**Google Adwords**
Book
Written By: Harry J. Misner

This book has been self-published & ghost written. So if you notice any grammatical errors or changes that you think should be made, please send an email to: **books@harrymisner.com**

I try to revise the book once every quarter until its perfect, and if you send me an email with proof of purchase & the recommended changes that need to be made, you'll receive the revised & updated PDF version of the book in a reply email when/if the change has been made FREE of Charge!


Part-1

Introduction
Adwords
Importance of Adwords
Getting Started
Writing Your Ads
Activate Your Account
Navigate Your Account
Landing Page
How can we Design a
Landing Page?

The Best Damn
**Google Adwords**
Book
Written By: Harry J. Misner

I0475397

## Part-2

## Part-3

**The Best Damn**
# Google Adwords
### Book

Written By: Harry J. Misner

## Introduction

Adwords is a highly lucrative profit-centre where I always earn a return to the tune of between 100-200%, on my investment by using a range of different products and affiliate campaigns. If you follow my guidelines and I will guarantee you that you will earn hefty profits in the shortest possible time, and within next few months, you may even start to earn four or five figure income. Adwords is Google's special and workable pay-per-click advertising program. It has become famous over the time and everyone ranging from "Google Cashers" (you will learn a lot about them in this book) to the largest of corporations who need to promote their brands use this program. To me, it is possibly one of the fastest and quickest ways to make a decent earning along with affiliate marketing. It is also quite simple and easy and hassle free to operate, once you learn and master the basic principles of this business opportunity. You can use other methods like search engine optimization, forum posting, and classified advertising in conjunction with this program.

In my earnest opinion, Adwords beats most of the similar programs, because you can extend this program to a number of other programs in the course of time.

The Adwords program allows advertisers (you) to buy keyword-enriched text and links on the Google results page. You will pay for the ad (based on selected keywords), only when someone clicks it and later visits your Web site. The amount of money you pay for each visitor can be as low as few cents or as high as $80. It depends on the quality of your ad and its keywords, the relevancy of your Web site, and the competitiveness of the prevailing market as defined and noted by the keyword or key word phase, typed by the web site visitor. Each text ad on the results page consists of 4 lines and up to 130 characters.

- **Line 1:** Blue color underlined hyperlinked headline containing up to 25 characters
- **Line 2:** Description line 1 of containing to 35 characters
- **Line 3:** Description line 2 containing to 35 characters
- **Line 4:** Green display URL (URL stands for Uniform Resource Locator, the way the Internet assigns calls Web sites) containing to 35 characters.

You are on your pathway to earn thousands of dollars right from the reading room of your own home.

This book provides you enough information on how you can start your own program. You just need two things to start an Adwords campaign:

☞ Five dollars
☞ A landing page

**A** landing page is the clickthrough destination of your web page, with the URL underlying your ad's link. Most advertisers using Google AdWords spend quite a bit more than five dollars, but that simple amount is all that Google requires activating your account.

# Adwords

An Adwords account contains three different sectors of operations

## Keywords

Keywords or its phrases are the terms people use to search for information, and they can trigger your ads over the internet. Almost every keyword has its own individual cost-per click value. Your chosen keywords are the most important component of your AdWords campaign. When you bid your money on the right keywords by using a targeted ad, and later direct your visitors to a highly relevant and useful landing page, you can increase the chances that your web site visitor will perform a desired action, like confirming a purchase, or filling out a lead form or even sign up for a newsletter.

The foundation of every successful AdWords campaign is the rock-solid and formidable keyword list. If you are bidding on the wrong keywords, it does not really matter how good your ad copy or landing page is, the user still may not click on your ad and purchase something. Even worse, you may also invite many unwanted or unqualified clicks, which can result in a costly campaign.

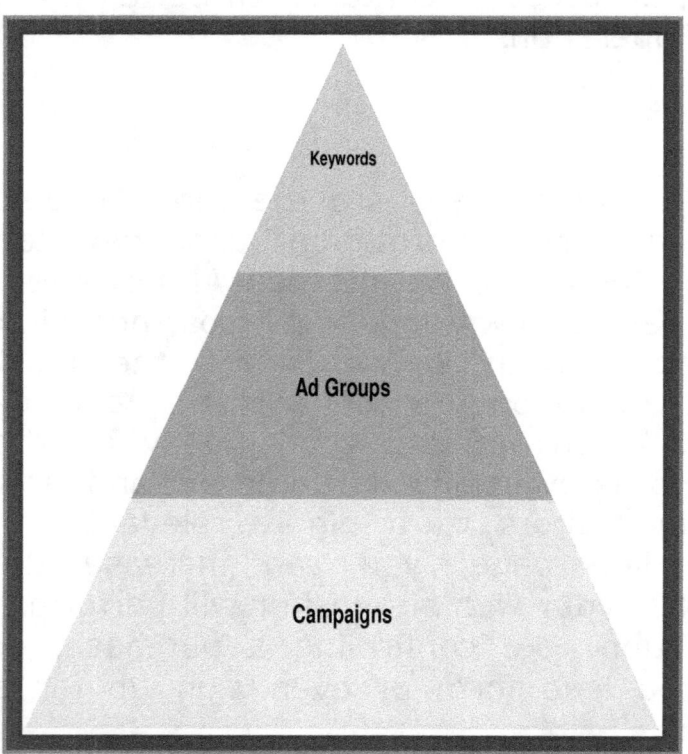

## Ad Groups

Ad Groups contain clusters of many keywords, each of which is related to one or more ads. Under each campaign, you can use several Ad Groups. Ad Groups are the holding bins for related ads and keywords and their phrases.

The best way to setup your ad groups is to place your keywords into highly related or connected categories.

For example, if you were promoting a company that sells coats, you may separate and distinguish your ad groups by product line connected to coats. You could then create a separate ad group for leather coats, one for silk, and one for cotton.

## Campaigns

Campaigns always contain different Ad Groups. Under the account level, you may have one or more different campaigns. For each campaign, you can limit your daily budget, language and geographic targeting, the types of web sites you want to advertise on, and, start and end dates for the campaign. You can even organize your campaigns in any way you want to.

Some of the more effective methods include hosting ads by geography (New York, Chicago, and London), language (English, Spanish, German), and distribution preference (search engines only, content sites only, or both search and content).

## Importance of Adwords

**1)** Developing new products is always time consuming, difficult and expensive. Pay per Click controls the way and manner media acts and performs. This activity takes almost 90% of the risk out of starting a new business or launching a new product or service. Now, you can test your ideas and vision in minutes, not days, weeks or months! Therefore, PPC is the best method to test your marketing.

**2)** Google Adwords can provide you instant results - you can float ad campaign within just 10 minutes. Compared to this, Yahoo can take anywhere from two to 5 days because the review process is always manual.

**3)** Google's perceived dominance in search helps you attract more visitors through Adwords, than any other pay per click platform. In fact, Google says that its reach extends to almost 80% of active Internet users.

**4)** Ads and keywords are instantly approved by Google and you can begin your work within few hours. This swiftness allows you to launch new campaigns without having to wait for editorial approval. Any changes or modifications that you make to your ad copy, keyword list, or landing page are also updated instantly.

**5)** Advertising is your investment, just like any other type of investments. It has to pay it, to make to more lucrative and profitable. Direct marketing is the art and science of making advertising pay for the desired results.

This is really a quick and crash course in direct marketing, by using Google Adwords as your prime advertising medium. Google Adwords is the fastest way to become a direct marketing master.

**6)** With the magic of Adwords, you can target your prospects on a geographical basis even down to countries, states and cities level. This is the greatest advantage for selling your products or services; you can now attract local prospects as opposed to someone living in a remote corner of the world.

**7)** There is no monthly minimum spending commitment here and no stipulate contract period as well.

**8)** You can settle your accounts only after the clicks have been recorded. It means that you pay only after the first 30 days.

**9)** You can determine the text of your ad and specify the type and number keywords for which your ad should be displayed.

**10)** You can even change the text of your ads at any time and at no extra cost.

## Getting Started

Google has a number of excellent guides and systematic directions that teach you how to open an account. Google also changes the appearance of its Adwords user interface from time to time and any printed reference materials book may become obsolete within no time.

Opening a new Adwords account is very easy, because Google has a very simple sign up and campaign procedure that you can do very easily.

Go to the following website to open your Adwords account at https://adwords.google.com/select/main?cmd=Login

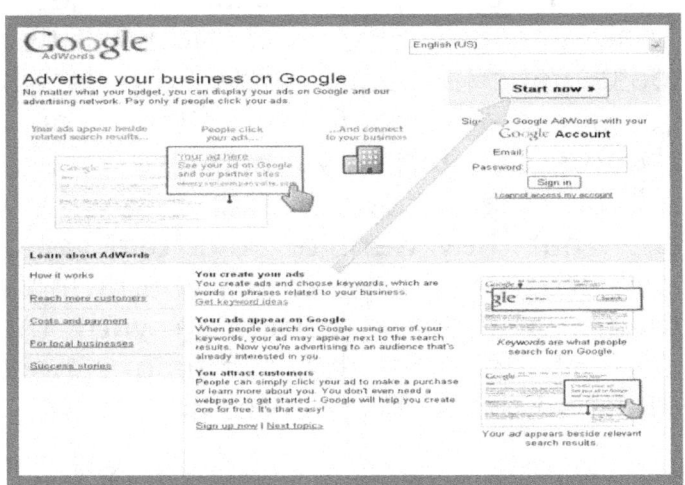

Never ever, open your Adwords account on a Friday or over the weekend because Google may take a few days for your account to be activated. Towards the middle of the screen, you will see a button that reads, "Sign up now -Click to Begin".

Upon clicking the "Sign up now" button, you will navigate to a screen, where you will click "Pick the solution that's right for you" button to go the next page. There are two options here, a "Starter edition" and a "Standard edition".

If you own an existing account, you can skip this section and start exploring three basic features of the Standard Edition: *campaign management, keyword selection, and ad writing.* In future, you will be using all these features and functionalities of Standard edition, so please choose this as your main account type.Later, you will be asked to choose your language. Now, this is where it can get somewhat confusing. When you create an Adwords account, you need to create your first ad, but many people do not have any idea or plan, what they want to advertise yet or how they can proceed. So what will you do now? You can create a "bogus" campaign with the sole intention of deleting the campaign, once you have finished the sign up process.

When you choose your Language, you will need to decide and confirm where you want your ads to appear. Because, you are creating a "bogus" campaign, there is no need to "hyper-target" your ads. You can simply choose to display the ads in "Countries and territories" of your choice.

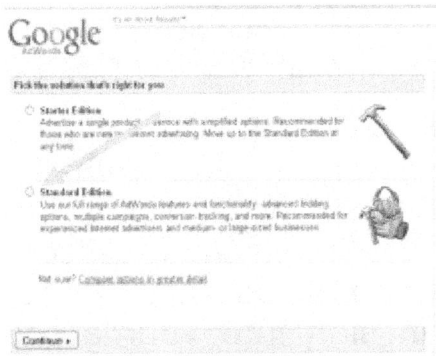

For signup process, if you have a Google account, then you can use it to create your Adwords account as well. If you do not have a Google account with you then you will need to sign up, by choosing the "Create a new Google Account, to be your login to Adwords".

Enter your e-mail address and password and press continue. You will now receive a confirmation email in you email inbox and it will include instructions on how to confirm and sign into your new Adwords account.

First, you will need to choose and select how you will pay for Adwords. Based on your IP address, Google automatically determines your local currency and the locality, and sets that as the default value, but you may wish to change it to US dollars. The most preferred currency is dollars. You cannot change or alter this setting, after activating your account.

Now, you are perfectly ready to create your first and new ad. Check your email box for the verification letter Google sends you after sign-up. Click on the link in the message to verify and confirm your email address. Once you confirm that, you can sign into your account and start creating your first ad.

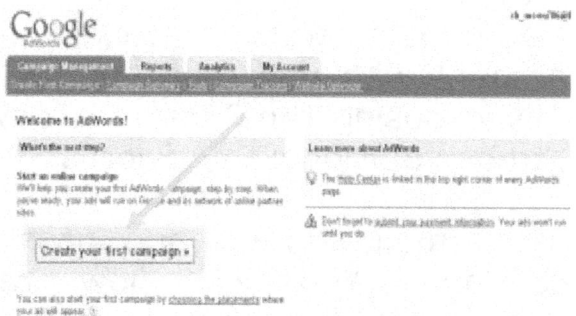

Select the country here you want your ads to appear by choosing in the available countries and territories list box, and then click the add button to copy your selection to the selected countries and/or territories list box.

Select multiple countries if you want your ads to appear in more than one country.

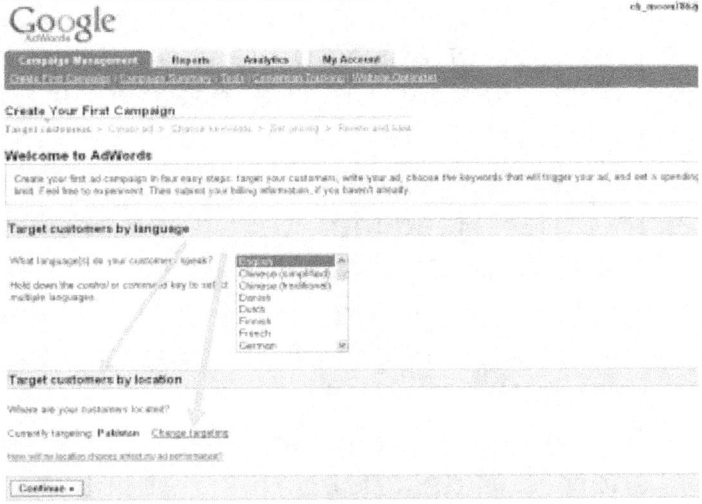

To remove a country or territory from the Selected Countries and/or Territories list box, select it and click the Remove button. When you are done, click the Continue button.

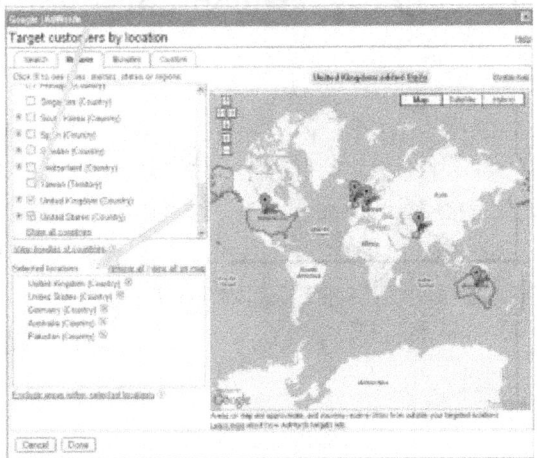

## Writing your Ads

Now, you can create your first ad. You can create any type of ads you want but be ready to change and tweak it in the near future. The following list provides some idea on what to enter in those text boxes:

- In the Headline text box, type the problem or opportunity.
- In the Description Line 1 text box, enter a short description of the main benefit of buying the product.
- In the Description Line 2 text box, write a short description about your product/service.
- In the Display URL text box, enter your Web site's name.
- In the Destination URL text box, enter the URL of the exact web page you want your customers to visit.

Type your chosen keywords into the list box and click the Continue button when you are finished. For now, just type a single keyword, for example, used cars, glow in the dark poker chips, functional fitness training.

Next to the box where you enter your keywords, you may choose to select more. If your URLs point to a working Web site, Google quickly scans the site and suggests you other keywords, based on your Web site copy and Google's database of related searches. If it cannot find your Web site, you can enter your main keyword and Google will give you a variation and related searches from its database.

The keyword-suggestion tool is quite beneficial. Until you learn and master how to create tightly focused ad groups, the tool may spoil your ad campaign. Use this tool later to refine and fine-tune your campaigns. Right now, just pick one or two closely related terms and continue.

When asked, "How much you would like to spend per day?" you can just enter $1.00 or the equivalent in your chosen currency. When asked, "The maximum you are ready to pay each time someone clicks on your ad?" you can enter $0.01, or the minimum bid that Google will allow you to enter.

**Y**ou will be asked to review your ad, choose whether you want to receive information from Google, and to specify where you heard about Google Adwords. Click "Continue.

**C**ongratulations! You are now one-step closer to starting your first advertising campaign. Read the next section to learn techniques that you can use to create Adwords campaigns that will out perform your competition, increase your traffic, and improve your overall Return on Investment.

## Activate Your Account

Are you ready to float your ad campaign? Click on the Activate Account button and complete the form.

### To activate your account:

### <u>Steps</u>:

- ✍ Use the drop-down list to select your billing country. The most common options are at the top, followed by long list of countries.

- ✍ Choose your country from the Time Zone Country or Territory dropdown list, and then select your time zone from the Time Zone dropdown list. Google will not let you change or edit your time zone once you have set it.

🕮 Enter the promotional code at the back of this book to recoup the cost of this book, in free clicks.

🕮 Click the Continue button.

🕮 Choose a payment method.

🕮 Accept Google's Terms and Conditions.

🕮 Click OK.

> Google always charges your credit card on a pay-as-you-click system. Cards accepted are JCB, American Express, MasterCard, or Visa.

Now, you will go to a screen, where you can fill out necessary billing information. Once you complete the form, your account will go live — and your ad should start displaying on the right side of the Google search results page. After you complete your account setup, wait for 15 minutes, and then do a search on your keyword. Look at the top and at the right of the search results page. If you do not see your ad, scroll down and click the More Sponsored Links link. Keep flipping the pages, until you see your ad or you go the end of the listings. This exercise gives you an idea of the competitiveness of your market. If you see many competitors, do not get discouraged.

# Navigate your Account

**1)** Campaign Management
**2)** Reports
**3)** Analytics
**4)** My Account
**5)** Billing Summary

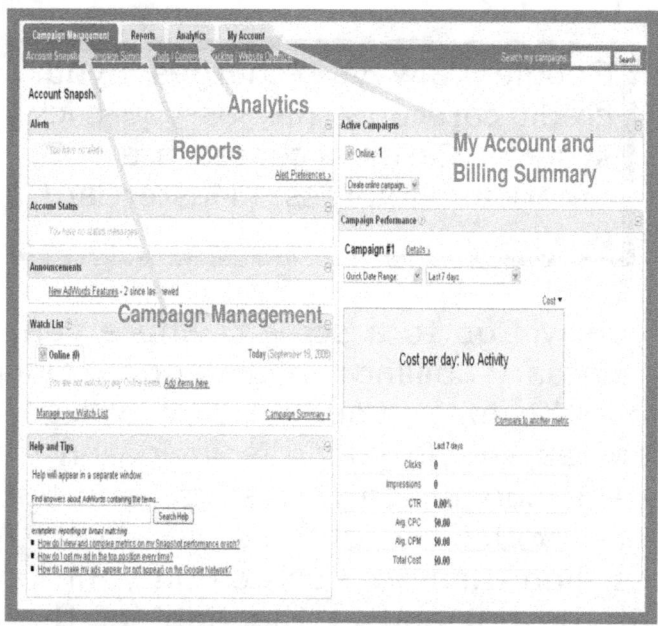

## 1) Campaign Management

Here, you can control all your costs, as well as your account, campaign, Ad Group, and keyword activity. The top most level displays your performance data for different campaigns. When you click on campaign, it shows Ad Group performance information, while clicking on an Ad Group displays keyword performance details.

## 2) Reports

This tab allows you to create and design customized and detailed reports by keyword, ad text, account, and other variables. Use a trial and error method by running different reports. Google can store up to five reports in your Download Center. Alternatively, you can instruct Google to mail them to your inbox.

## 3) Analytics

This tab gives you advanced tools to track your campaign results and other related data.

## 4) My Account

Use this tab to control all your personal information, such as your login information and user preferences. Here, you can find billing information.

## 5) Billing Summary

The Billing Summary page will display only the high-level items, such as charges, credits, and end-of-month balances. For every month, you can check how many times you were charged, and for the amount.

## Landing Page

This section applies to those advertisers who have decided to create their own landing page and not just routing the traffic to the merchant. You can try this out to see if you can conversion ratios. Depending upon the type of product you are promoting, the landing page could ask the user to do any one of the following:

- Subscribe to a newsletter
- Buy a product
- Download trial software

Back in the year 2006, Google had enforced their policy to rate the quality of the landing page, also known as the "Google Slap". Many people hated this change in policy, as the prices of bids increased in an alarming manner. However, there are two significant advantages here:

- The competition was completely silenced. People who were on the right side of the fence created many profits, as their CPC became very affordable.
- It gives you another advantage and once you know how to do this, it can become your useful feature.

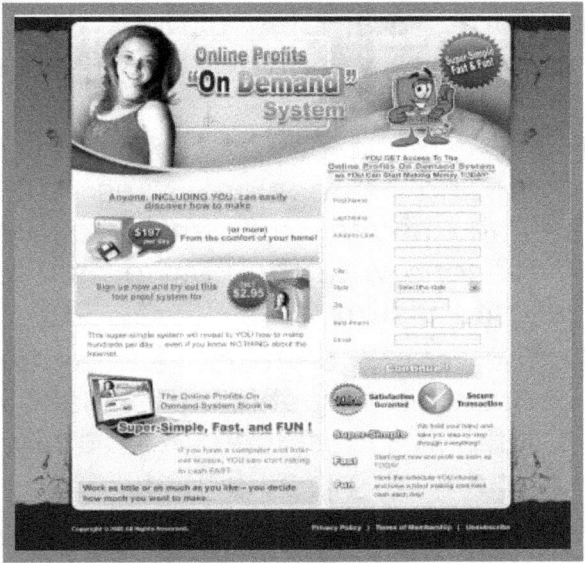

## Features

You will need to convince an end-user to purchase a specific product or may encourage a web site visitor to fill out an online form for generating a lead. This action is highly desirable and it called a "conversion". The efficiency or quality of your landing page is a measure of the conversion rate of visitors into definite and positive actions.

Landing pages come handy for use in Pay per Click PPC campaigns, and is a very good way to monitor the effectiveness of your paid ads. By supplementing parameters to the linking of URL, you can now compare effectiveness of ad based on relative click-through rates.

Here are some examples of how you can use landing pages with various traffic sources:

- Traffic from a pay per click (PPC) search marketing campaign goes to multiple landing pages efficiently optimized to correspond with the keywords used by the web site visitor.
- Traffic can go from a banner ad or sponsorship graphic to a landing page specifically designed to address that particular target audience.

## How do you Design a Landing Page?

When you want to design a landing page, ensure the following:

- Include all possible critical elements in the upper 300 pixels areas of the page: Usability research of the past shows over half of your site visitors will NOT scroll "below the fold." Area. So, just forget the idea of a warm-up copy, ensure that you are getting straight to the point, and keep your value proposition at first screen view. Headlines, in particular ones that have a larger text or are included within <h1> tags should be highly relevant and related and should include the keywords taken from the search query.

✍ Think simple and straight! Use a one-column format with ample margins and white space to increase readability. Break up big paragraphs into smaller chunks — and not more than five lines. Encourage visitors to read, attract, and engage them with your message. Dense or gaudy looking copy does not get audience.

✍ Within the <title></title> tags on your webpage, you should also include the keywords that were used in the search query. If someone typed in "find red flowers" and you may wish to ensure that it is the exact phrase.

✍ Be obvious and use standard usage patterns of the industry: Underline your links, be clear, descriptive and specific when you are describing them. Visitors should not waste their time on your page or understand your message.

✍ Make sure your page loads quickly: Dial up is still the preferred internet connection. Depending on your marketing and your product/service needs, try for an eight-second or less page upload. Never ever, fill your page with unnecessary graphics and images.

🖎 Optimize essential graphics and images to reduce overall file size and load time.

🖎 Format and design your page according to the F-Pattern Eye-Tracking Principle: Web readers tend to track or glance through the web page content in a rough F-shaped pattern. So, always format important images and graphics on to the left side of the page.

🖎 Use the similar color palette/visual elements from your ads on your landing page: Ensure a smooth, consistent flow of design elements to help keep your prospect fixed on your web pages and also assure that they are right on your lading page.

🖎 Do not use things like clip art! Choose a single dominant and prominent photo image to be your main theme: Use a product photo. Make it clickable and do not forget to add n attractive and cajoling caption.

🖎 Put your message, copy or image, almost very close to the middle of your page.

## Part-2

## Keyword Research

Your customers create one of the most critical online strategies on your behalf; the keywords that your consumers use are the biggest asset to your business. Your main duty is not to invent or find the new keywords, but to detect and find out about the keywords that a typical web user is using. Finding good keywords is the last key to your AdWords success; if you cannot do that, your AdWords adventure is as good as dead. Without any good keywords, you cannot expect impressions, clicks, leads or sales. With careful planning, you can come out with a number of keywords that a number of people are searching right now.

Obviously, keywords are the most important components of your campaign. When you bid on the right type of keywords and later create a meaningful Google ad, you can definitely drive lot of traffic to your landing page. It means that your web users will perform a desirable action after clicking your Google advertisement. The foundation of a successful Google AdWords campaign is a formidable keyword list. Wrong keywords mean very disappointing conversion and utter waste of money.

Wrong keywords also mean that lot of unwanted site visitors will click on your ad link. The most important issue that you should consider while creating a campaign is to bid on highly specific keywords directly related to your products or services. On the other hand, the most foolish mistake that one can do is to bid on popular keywords at a high price but fail to convert them into sales because of wrong strategy.

When people want information, they also tend to use general and broad type of keywords and their phrases. As they mature, they start using more specific and highly targeted keywords for their searches. In fact, they use such keywords that they can easily find the products or services they want in seconds. You will need to find such keywords for your AdWords campaign.

For example, let us assume that you have a very good company that sells flowers. You know their web site by heart and you know how they sell their products. Now, try to know business strategies and in what manner they write web content to attract customers. The content on their web site will have important keywords. List those keywords that you think are very important and critical to their business. Now, you will see how people use such keywords to search products on this web site.

Here are some example and keywords and their phrases that people might use:

- ☞ flowers
- ☞ Flowers online
- ☞ Fresh flowers
- ☞ Seasonal fresh flowers
- ☞ Annual fresh flowers
- ☞ Fresh red flowers
- ☞ Fresh pink flowers
- ☞ Fresh flower seeds

The longer your list the better it will be, because the more number of keyword phrases you have, the more volume of visitors you can attract and the more conversion rate you can ensure. You will find that many of the most popular keywords are overpriced and too expensive.

Never ever, allow these trends discourage your confidence. You can invite click-traffic for much lower prices. Most advertisers think too narrowly and in a negative manner, bidding only on the most popular and hit words, which obviously inflates the price. Nevertheless, with a little effort you can identify and detect hundreds of keywords that cost only 5 to 10 cents per click.

> The key is in your keyword research. Check out every combination of keywords that are good.

Let us consider our fresh flower examples. Now, the minimum bid on Google for the term *fresh flowers* is $1.45. That is the minimum bid price; you may wish to continue with your research until you find a list of keyword combinations costing only five cents.

## Tips to Find Keywords and Combinations

☞ Try the plural versions of the keyword
☞ Try different verbal forms of the keyword – buy, buying, etc.

- ☞ Use combined keywords without including spaces, for example instead of fresh flowers.
- ☞ Always use synonyms, word substitutes, and similar words.
- ☞ Include brand names and different models of products sold.

## Keyword Formats

Adwords uses three different types of phrase matches to fityour ads with the terms searched at the time. These include:

- ✎ Broad Match (without quotes or brackets),
- ✎ Phrase Match (with quotes)
- ✎ Exact Match (with square brackets)

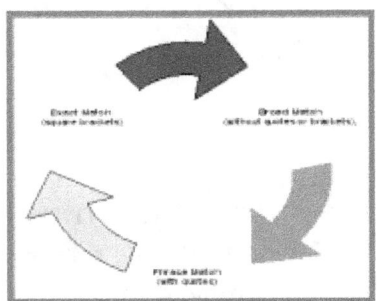

## Broad match

This is the default option of Google AdWords. When you include keyword phrases such as fresh flowers in your keyword list, your ads will appear on the search engine, when web users search for fresh and flowers, in any order and possibly along with other terms like red fresh flowers, fresh flowers for wedding, and so on. These matches are low target keyword phrases than exact or phrase matches.

## Phrase Match

Your ad will appear on the search engine pages when web users search on the exact phrase and when their search consists of additional terms, as long as the keyword phrase is in exactly the same sequential order. A phrase match for "fresh flowers" will appear when a user searches on: red fresh flowers, pink fresh flowers, but not for: flowers for birthday.

## Exact Match

The search query performed must exactly match your keyword. This means [fresh flowers] will only match: fresh flowers and not for: red fresh flowers, even if the second part of the query contains your keyword.

## Tips for Using Keyword Formats Options

✍ If you are not sure which keyword matching option to use, then enter all three variations in your keyword list. For example:
Fresh flowers
"Fresh flowers"
[Fresh flowers]

Now, you can compare the click through rates of the three keywords and then later remove one or two that are ineffective and useless. You can also reduce the possibility of your Ad Group being turned off by Google because of very low click through rates.

✍ As a newbie, you should always use the "broad match keywords" type of keyword matching option when you have limited budget. You should only use the "phrase match" and "exact match" keyword matching options when you see that there are no real click through rates.

✍ Specific keywords are costlier to bid because the web users who search for these terms are always on target.

✍ Google's Keyword Tool will tell you which similar keyword terms your "broad match keywords" will appear.

✎ You can enter broad match keywords as negative keywords in Ad Group if and when necessary, e.g., when you want to use "flowers" but not "flower sales" and "flower seller."

## Use Dynamic Keywords

You can use dynamic keywords to get keywords that are more relevant into your ad group. With dynamic keywords, you can create a placeholder somewhere inside your ad text. Now, Google automatically places your keywords into that placeholder, when a web user searches for that keyword.

For example, let us say that you have an ad group that promotes different products. The outline of the ad may look similar for all these products. The only visible variable that would change will be the product title. It is almost impossible for anyone to create ads for each of these products. Nevertheless, with dynamic keyword insertion, you can make sure the title of the product appears in every ad, every time the web user searches for it. To use the facility of dynamic keywords, you should use a special syntax in the ad text. First, determine and find out where you want your keywords to appear in your ad text.

Later, use the keyword placeholder to insert your keyword into the ad text.

For example,

{Keyword: Default Ad Text}

The curly braces represent the beginning and end of your keyword.

{Keyword} New keyword will come here from your ad group.

Default ad text: This is the display text entered when Google cannot use your keyword in the copy.

For the purpose of illustration,

Let us say that you wanted to use dynamic keyword insertion in your headline for a bouquet of fresh flowers that exceeded the 25-character limit.

Now, Google cannot insert the title of the product on your behalf, but will use the default ad text instead. In the example, it uses a placeholder like {Keyword: buy fresh flowers}.

## Keywords Strategies

If your ad campaign is perfect, every click leads to a sale, and you may never miss any clicks that *could* have led to a confirmed sale. However, a perfect campaign is never possible by anyone. Selection of keywords is a delicate act of balancing hyper-aggressive and hyper-conservative approaches:

## 1) Hyper-aggressive

If you are too aggressive and select every possible keyword, you may not miss anyone over the internet. However, the CTR obtained will be too small and tiny. Above all, the bid price will be too much.

## 2) Hyper-conservative

If you bid only on the obvious keywords, you will miss many sales resulting from people click on sensitive keywords. You may wish to create a balance your strategy with one that maximizes your overall business goals. Your business goals should be focusing on handsome profits.

You may also sacrifice some amount of profits for the highest ROI. To increase ROI, you may wish to consider the following:

> Start your campaign with the obvious keywords. Create a list of the keywords that any web user will search on Google

> Now, you can also create a list of phrases and synonyms. Employ Google Keyword Search Tool to conduct the research.

> Change and edit underperforming keywords and keep looking for better ones. Part III of this book shows you how to manage your Adwords campaigns to improve your results.

## How to Write Ads

Writing ads is the hardest part of Adwords to learn, understand and master. On the other hand, you will know what works better and what does not immediately, because your clicks will tell you about the success of the campaign.

The best method to see which ads bring you the best CTR is to write down three or four ads at one time. Later check for the success of your clicks. Ads with the highest clickthrough rate (the number of clicks divided by the number of times ad displayed) are the best performers.

Here are some simple techniques explained by seasoned Adwords veterans:

- Include important keywords in your ad headline, since that is what people will be looking for and it makes your ad seem more fit and relevant.

- Relate your ad to the theme and content on your website. Thus, you can enhance the CTR.

- Get to the point and be specific. Include the most relevant information about your business. Let it be concise, and encourage the user to take immediate action.

Every Adwords ad consists of four rows.

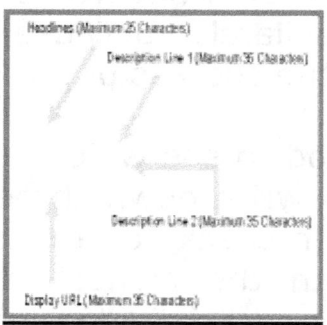

## Headlines

The best headlines are those that directly relate to the keywords searched. They make your ad seem more relevant to the web user's interests. The ad text will become bold when a word or a phrase in your ad text is identical to the keyword. The headline is very critical because you can take three times more effort as long to write the headline than the actual ad text itself.

If your headline cannot grab attention of web users, then the ad text becomes useless and irrelevant. Moreover, some people just display the headline and not the ad text. Thus, it is important dedicate your time and effort to create a meaningful headline. Google only offers 25 characters for to create your headline.

### Google's Guidelines for the Headline

Google requires that all headlines meet certain important rules and specifications. Following are the most important: Superlatives are avoided, e.g. "The Fastest delivery" or "The Quickest PC Shipping." You cannot use any general instructions, e.g. "Click Here" or "Call Now" (no telephone number in the ad text). Google does not allow X-rated or objectionable content.

## Descriptions

The description must convey both the benefits of using your product and the call to a positive action. Let it be everything as short and simple as you can. To start with, list your products and its benefits. Then, combine with an immediate call to action.

Writing profitable ad description means that the reader must not only be convinced, but also motivated enough to click on your ad and purchase a product. The reader must believe that you have something of worth to offer.

***Here are some tips for writing ad descriptions***

- ☞ Analyze and evaluate your product or service
- ☞ Turn all features into possible benefits
- ☞ Position your product or service in the market
- ☞ Define and explain your target group
- ☞ Highlight benefits and avoid listing features
- ☞ Create an incentive or reward
- ☞ Avoid word games, pun and humor

## Google's Guidelines for the Ad Text

The Adwords program requires compliance with a number of rules on how to write ad text. These are the most important and critical for your campaign. If your ad text includes prices or discounts, you must display them clearly on your website within 1-2 clicks. The same policy applies to advertising claims made by you in comparing your products to those of your competition. If you are targeting your ad on regional basis, then you should identify this in the ad text, by naming the region. If you are a partner in a partner program, you must identify this properly in the ad text, e.g. with "(Partner)," "(Affiliate)," "Aff" or "subsidiary." Do not place any ads for online casinos, online gambling or dialer programs. Online pharmacies must be a certified member of the Square Trade Licensed Pharmacy program (only available for pharmacies within the U.S. and Canada).

## <u>Display & Destination URLs</u>

The Display URL (web address) does not have to be similar as your Destination URL. Nevertheless, it should be an actual URL of your site. Choose a Destination URL that signifies the exact product or service that your audience is searching for, rather than your usual homepage.

Your home page is usually most effective in directing or leading your potential clients to the landing page. The display URL is the third important part of an Adwords ad apart from the headline and the ad text. Some people even claim that the display URL is the most conspicuous and visible part of the ad because it stands out clearly in the color green. Google does not allow you to use a display URL significantly different from that of your destination URL. You can also make the display URL short.

http://www.freshflowers-123.net/products/redfreshflowers.html
You can simply enter the following:
www.redfreshflowers-123.net

## Split Testing in Adwords

One very important point to consider with headlines (and the body of the ad too) is split testing. Split testing means placing two of your ads head to head in the same ad group. You will let ads run until one of them is quite clearly the better of the two (wait for 20-30 clicks before making a decision), and then you take the winner and pit it against another of your ads - repeatedly.

Tip: Use www.splitester.com

Why do we that we should test the copy for at least '30 click'? In fact, it is not simply a number but a scientific estimate. You can use an excellent online tool that helps you in this direction. Split testing is necessary, if you want to improve your ad copy. The main goal here is not to make rapid or quick changes, but small measurable and visible ones so that you can make out which change actually causes improvements in CTR. This way, you can easily determine the type of ads that work best for your niche and thus create effective, compelling ads.

## Launching Adwords Campaign

If you followed the instructions in the section "Setting up an Adwords Account" you will already have a "Bogus" or false account that you will need to delete in the meantime. Once you delete this campaign, you can create a new one by using the techniques and methods given below.

To achieve immense success with Adwords, you will need to learn and understand how to create campaigns, ad groups, effective ad copy and the right techniques for bidding and finding correct keywords.

All of these simple, yet time confusing tasks need to be done correctly in order to beat your competition and later create a positive Return on Investment (ROI). It is very easy to create a campaign, but making it work on the ground could be very difficult.

## Step-1

First, you need to name your campaign in a proper manner. For example, you could call your campaign "fresh flowers" and use it to promote freshflowers.com. The main reason for having a proper naming scheme is to ensure better organization of your multiple accounts and their keywords.

## Step-2

When you create your campaign, you can use your own settings as per the needs and requirements. In the first section (Setting up an Adwords account), there are screenshots of how you can set up your campaign, but now you will learn how you can effectively set up a real campaign. When you set up a campaign the first thing you should do is turn off the Content network. The reason you want to do this is that for a majority of products you host on this network you may not see any conversion.

However, you can still get a lot of traffic, but the quality of the traffic is usually from Adsense that is full of click fraud and untargeted and useless traffic. So, turn the content network off, and leave the Search network instead

**Step-3**

When you first set up your Adwords campaign, you will chose from various targeting options. You can select options in the Edit Campaign Settings page within your Adwords account.

## Language Settings

You can reach and connect to people in over 40 languages. However, you must write your ads and keywords in the language of your choice (Google will not translate). If you are targeting on multiple languages, you can set up a new campaign for each one, although you can choose to run ads in all or any number of these languages.

## Geographic Settings

It is possible to set individual campaigns to target and reach searchers living in a particular country/territory, regional, city or customized level. If you chose regional, city, or customized targeting, you may need to add a counterpart country or territory-targeted campaign.

Even if you can offer products or services only to people living within a very specific geographic area, a broader and wide campaign can help you get clicks that are more qualified from your prospective customers on Google and its partner sites.

**Step-4**

## Create a Daily Budget

Once you add your keywords, you are ready to setup a daily budget for the said campaign. Remember to start with a conservative and small budget. A good rule is not spending more than you can afford to lose; it is a simple guideline! Once the campaign is up and running for a few days, you will have a better understanding of the budget required to manage and run your campaign.

## Set Click Pricing

After you have setup a budget for campaign, you can set your maximum cost per click for the selected keywords. By default options, you can set one maximum cost per click for all of the keywords in the ad group. However, you can change individual keyword's max cost per click before the campaign. You will also notice that Google gives you cost estimates after you submit your budget and set pricing options for your keywords.

These estimates are accurate with Google Adwords, but your costs could be significantly higher or lower depending on a number of factors. Now, you can submit your campaign for a final review when you feel that all parameters are working and to your complete satisfaction.

## Step-5

### Ad Group

The next step is to create an Ad that allows you to organize your keywords. The success of your campaign is directly affected by how your Ad Groups perform. Thus, it is very important to create them in a proper manner. In order to create a highly efficient campaign, you will need to create tightly targeted and better-focused Ad Groups with a small amount of relevant keywords embedded in each. You can use up to 25 unique keywords per Ad Group.

For example, you can promote a flower selling site and you can name your campaign as `fresh flowers`. You should now create a new campaign for each promotion; make sure that run an organized campaign, especially when you spend a lot of time and effort. Be sure to give your campaign a name that people can recognize and remember.

**W**ithin your campaign, you can create and set up multiple Ad groups. An ad group is a list of related keywords for which you will be displaying the same ads. It is better to have lot of ad groups (as many as 50) within each campaign, and 5-20 keywords within each ad group (for a fully rolled out campaign).

Do not promote too many ad groups though there are advertisers with 500+ ad groups within a campaign. You may limit to a maximum of a 15 and 50 per group.

**I**n order to create highly relevant Ad Groups, it is very important to group your keywords together using the "Common" keyword method. If all keywords have at least one common word, you will be able to use this word in your ad copy.

For example;

- ☞ flowers
- ☞ fresh flowers online
- ☞ fresh flowers seasonal
- ☞ red fresh flowers
- ☞ seasonal fresh flowers
- ☞ pink fresh flowers
- ☞ fresh flowers wedding
- ☞ fresh flowers birthday
- ☞ fresh flowers seeds

Adwords can calculate and assess the quality of your ad based on a number of factors. Google calls this the "Quality Score" and it plays a very important role in the positioning and overall effectiveness of your ads. The higher the rate of CTR, the better and result oriented your quality score will be. The bigger your Quality score is, the fewer amounts you will pay per click, and the higher position your ad will be within the search results.

## Quality Score

Experts and professionals talk a lot about Google's new quality score algorithm. In the past, a keyword or ad position was determined by their CTR and the maximum cost per click. Now, Google looks at the landing page and keywords with the relevancy and theme of your business. To determine your overall quality score, all you need to do is click on your campaign, and then your ad group. By default, the quality score column is turned off, so we do not know what our quality score is for these keywords. If we click on the customized column link, we can show or hide any column.

**N**ow Google will show us the quality score for each or our keywords. Let us learn what each of these scores mean and what the different grades are.

There are three different grades, great, satisfactory and poor. If your quality score has a great tag that means that you will pay less amount per click and your keyword is almost relevant.

| Google | | | | | | Actual CPC |
|---|---|---|---|---|---|---|
| Advertiser | Max CPC | Quality Score | Rank # | Position | Min Bid | Actual CPC |
| A | $0.40 | 1.8 | 0.72 ($0.40 x 1.8) | 1 | $.04 | $0.37 |
| B | $0.65 | 1.0 | 0.65 ($0.65 x 1.0) | 2 | $.05 | $0.39 |
| C | $0.25 | 1.5 | 0.38 ($0.25 x 1.5) | 3 | $.04 | $0.04 |

It means that your keyword or ad is very relevant, but you can still benefit from higher quality score. When your keyword is poor, Google means that your keyword is not very relevant to your ad and you need to improve your quality score in order to to continue to run your ad, or they will penalize you by raising your minimum cost per click. Google also offers some practical tips and suggestions for improving your quality score.

## Content Network

Content targeting is an automated process, using which you can control where your ads appear or appear across content sites.

Site Targeting gives you tools to search thousands of sites in Google network and choose the ones where you would like to place your ads. The Google content network comprises of hundreds of thousands of high-quality websites, news pages, and blogs that partner with Google to display targeted Adwords ads. When you choose to advertise on the content network, you can expand your marketing and advertizing reach to highly targeted audiences--and potential customers who visit these sites every day. There is no larger or bigger network for contextual advertising in the world than Google Content network.

**T**hese partner sites include:

- ☞ The New York Times
- ☞ About.com
- ☞ MarthaStewart.com
- ☞ Many smaller niche sites covering thousands of topics

Using Content Network may result in you loosing lot of money as more than 70% traffic comes through this network. However, if you have experience with Adwords and have enough campaign data and statistics, you can easily leverage the power of Content Network to promote your Google ads to increase your profits.

The content network consists of a large network of publishers that display different Google Ads on their web pages. Depending on the page content, Google will serve the most targeted set of ads on these sites. Theoretically, this traffic sounds highly targeted and focused. However, this traffic comes in the form of Arbitrage sites, and other bulk, low quality traffic strategies.

This perceived traffic simply does not convert the same way that a search network does, and it is suggested that you have this utility turned off in the initial process.

**Conversion Tracking**

Conversion Tracking is Google's special answer to third-party software packages that identify and trace traffic through a site. Specialized programs provide a more detailed picture than Google by giving information on from where traffic comes from, how it goes through the site, and the manner in which it exits. Google's tool can track how many click through visitors get through a simple conversion process at the landing site. Ordinarily, a customer who clicks on Adwords ad will be asked to carry out some sort of action on the landing page.

If you are an advertiser who needs traffic, than the issue of conversion does not raise at all. However, a business owns a landing page that gears itself towards collecting a simple signup or selling a product. On the other hand, affiliate marketers may face a situation when conversion tracking does not work.

Implementing conversion tracking in your account is quite simple; however, you need to have some knowledge of HTML code, at least to the level of cutting and pasting necessary codes into a Web page's source document. After you alter the document, you may wish to upload it to the site's server. Google provides you the necessary code. Here is a brief description of conversion tracking in action:

**1.** You will paste Google's code (which is a JavaScript) into the page that needs active tracking. This page is not the initial landing page per se, but the page, a web user lands on *after* performing an action. Therefore, the code may appear in a "Thank You" page soon after a newsletter sign-up request or a confirmed sale.

**2.** Google tracks web users as they start clicking through ads and land on the advertiser's site.

**3.** If the web user performs the necessary conversion action and comes to the post conversion page, Google's JavaScript will record this activity.

**4**. Google also reports conversion-tracking statistics in your Control Center. Google offers two basic versions of conversion tracking: *basic and customized*. The customization activity mostly consists of the ability to fix a price value for a product, so Google can carry out ROI statistics on your Control Center pages.

Most advertisers who are strange to conversion tracking may start with the basic version, which does a good job of tracking the number of click through that end up on the post-conversion page. This basic statistic is very critical in finding out your ROI and the effectiveness of Adwords system. To set up your account for basic conversion tracking, follow these simple steps:

> ✎ Click on the Campaign Management tab
> ✎ Click on Conversion Tracking button
> ✎ Under Basic Conversion Tracking, click on the Learn more links.
> ✎ Click on the Start tracking button.

**S**elect a language now and set your site's security level.

If you run a secure commerce site, the security level on the post-conversion page will be *https://* If not, your page's prefix is the regular *http://*

**5.** Copy the JavaScript code now and paste it into your post-conversion page.

## How Can We Find Target Market?

Most people will not have any idea where to find the prospective customers for their products. As a result, they simply fail in their Google AdWords marketing that focuses on selling good products. Not only can this be extremely frustrating, but also it ends up in wasting lot of precious time and money!

Log on to www.askhowie.com/freewords, type a keyword into the search box, and click Research. Now, you will see a long list of the top 100 keywords that also include the one you typed just now. Select and copy the entire list, including search volume numbers and paste the data on an Excel spreadsheet. You will see one column of numbers and another of keywords. Now, scan all keywords and delete any rows unrelated and unconnected to your market. For example, if you sell books on fresh flowers to flower growers, you can remove terms like Queen Rose from the list.

Inspect the remaining keywords, while paying attention to a number of things like:

☞ Keywords that are more popular (higher on the list) than others

☞ Are there just a few important keywords that result in a majority of searches?

☞ Do some of the keywords represent secondary markets within the main market?

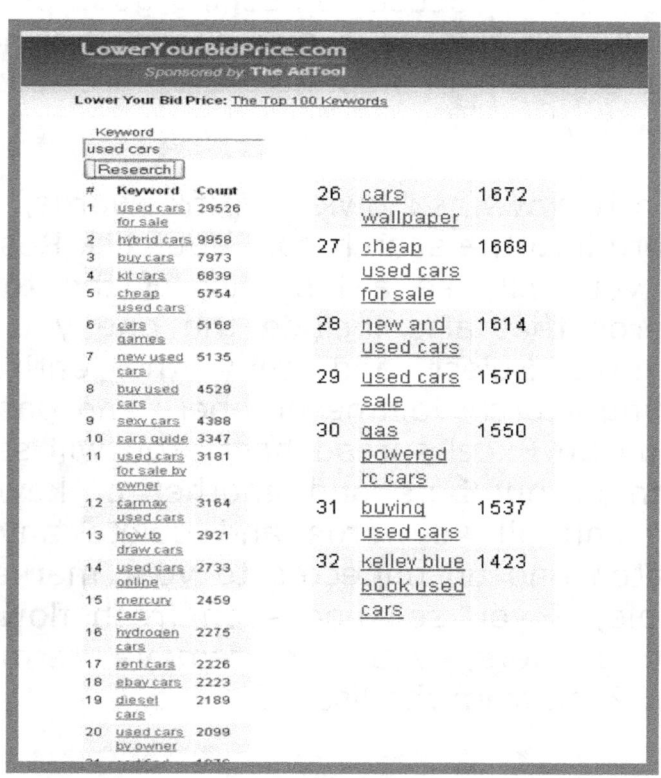

The total volume of searches for the top 100 keywords, appearing at the bottom of the page, is a viable indicator to know of if it is a good market to enter. Newbie Adwords marketers should focus on 500 and 5,000 searches per month (which translates almost into 50,000– 1,500,000 typical Google searches).

After you reach some success in less competitive but still lucrative markets, you can work on markets with 5,000 monthly searches or more by using the free keyword tool.

You can find a profitable niche in the USA that is under-exploited in the UK or Europe, later setup your AdWords campaign for those countries. If you want to host a foreign ad, you will need to write them in the foreign language. If you cannot write an ad in a foreign ad, you can seek the help of a language translation professional to write them.

Targeting a specific country is quite easy as well. You just need to select the country while you are carrying out your campaign. People run campaign in a number of countries like UK, Germany, France, Canada, Australia, Spain, Japan and others.

## How Can We Choose the Product and Converts It into Profitable?

Affiliate programs offer you a fantastic opportunity to sell a number of products. Here are some ideas on how to select a good affiliate program for AdWords promotion.

Before you sell affiliate products, you must first know how to distinguish good products from the bad ones. Choosing a product to promote or affiliate can be a very difficult proposition, especially when you do not know the type of products to choose. When selecting a product for affiliating, it is also very important that you perform thorough research. Researching a specific product will greatly benefit you, as you begin advertising and driving plenty of traffic to the site. The following are the methods that use to determine whether the product will be profitable to sell, and if it is of high quality.

### Step-1

This is not the best and recommended option for everyone, as it is very expensive to purchase every product that you try to promote. However, by purchasing a product you will be able to review the product first hand and pass on detailed features of the product to your website visitors.

This will translate into greater volume sales as you will learn the tricks of the trade and by understanding the product, you can detect and identify your target audience much easier.

If you do not have money to purchase the product, you can obtain product information by using other methods. You can study about what others are saying about it on a number of forums, blogs, and focus groups.

You can also look and see how other affiliates are reviewing the product and what they have reviewed about it. You can use these alternate techniques for obtaining product information without purchasing it.

## Step-2

If you are researching about a product, you should definitely look to see what other affiliates are doing, and what type of keywords they are promoting in the market. Type a search query into Google by using the keywords. Take note of the affiliate websites that are under the search terms. Typically, the more affiliates under a search term, the more money to be made within a particular industry. For example, let us say that you are promoting a product to help a wedding party to buy some fresh flowers.

If you search "fresh flowers" within Google and you get a list of affiliate websites promoting "fresh flowers" products under the paid listings, chances are some of these people are making decent amounts of money.

You can also confirm the profitability of these keywords by watching the Ads If the same websites are still appearing under that listing even after two weeks from the time you perform your original search, they are obviously making money.

**Step-3**

This is not the "be all- end all" for determining whether you should promote or not, but you can get a good idea of the number of web site users who visit any particular website, by checking its Alexa Ranking. Go to Alexa.com and type in the URL of the site that you want and check the information.

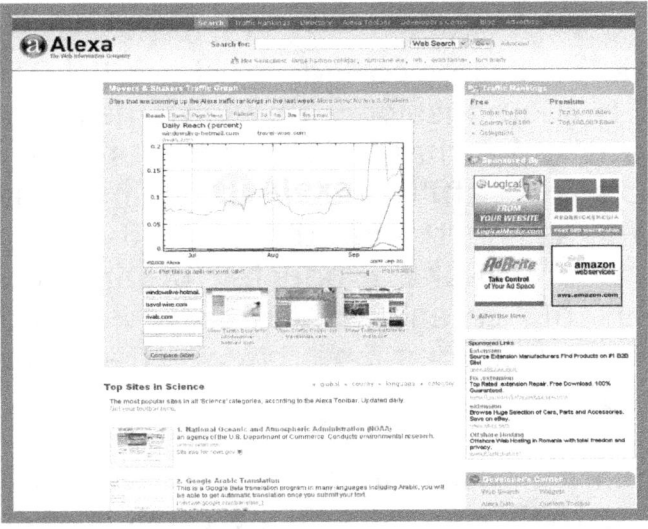

Alexa will asset find out the sites that receive the most traffic. For example, if you do a simple search for Beating Adwords, it is ranked roughly 50,000th in terms of incoming traffic.

Any website that shows traffic under the value of 100,000, it means that it receives a healthy volume of visitors. With this, you can determine that a number of affiliates are marketing that product. High traffic sites that offer affiliate programs are usually VERY profitable to promote and market. If possible, you can even create your own affiliate product and promote it on your web pages. Connect your affiliate web pages with Google AdWords to drive traffic to the landing page.

## Step-4

Affiliate program providers like ClickBank.com and CJ (Commission Junction) have a "New Merchant" area that lists merchants that provide products for affiliating and their commission rates for selling the product. Clickbank.com has their Information Products organized by a number of categories. Browse through the different categories and check the commission patterns.

You learn how to use Clickbank.com and promote their products. They provide an easy to use interface, and starting on the program is quick and simple. Once you sign up for a clickbank account, you can start promoting product announced in the network. A product with a high gravity, commission and volume means that a number of affiliates are making money by selling the product.

Clickbank uses four criteria to organize their products.

☞ Net Amount Earned
☞ Average Percentage Per Sale
☞ Referred
☞ Gravity

Gravity is the popularity of a particular product and is calculated by the number of different affiliates that have sold the product. If the product has a high gravity (50+) it means that, many affiliates have had immense success selling the product.

This is a very good indicator of how well the product is selling in the market. By using the $Earned/Sale and a formula outlined below, you can determine the rate of refunds for a given product. Along with Gravity, it will help you find whether the product is worth advertising.

From time to time, an affiliate can face the piquant situation when the buyer returns the product for a refund. You can use the following formula to calculate the refund rate of a product, and help determine the overall customer satisfaction.

(Product Price - 7.5%) - $1 = Post CB Commission

Post CB Commission x Payout Percentage = Affiliate Commission

Affiliate Commission - $Earned/Sale = Refund Difference

($Refund Difference ÷ Affiliate Commission) x 100 = Refund Percentage

Some products have a very high refund rate, the rate being over 20%. Please be careful while promoting products with a refund rate of over 20%, because your Return on Investment will be quite low due to poor customer satisfaction and products with a questionable quality.

If the return on investment is good, even after the refunds, you may want to continue to promote that product; but this will be a personal decision on your part. It is possible to promote products with over a 50% refund rate; however, it could be a big risk.

You may never want to spend $10 to make just $1 profit. Products with high refund rates will always yield very low Return on Investment, sometimes lower than 100%.

If a product gives you 100% ROI, it means that you are currently spending $10 in advertising and promotion to make $20 (with $10 net profit). Consider campaigns that yield 100% ROI to achieve success. Understanding how to set up your Adwords campaign will play a big role in your success.

There are several ways of making money:

- You should focus on doing well in this business. Gravity level for a number of products is very high and you can use this indicator to sell good products. Product with very high gravity values mean better affiliating opportunity.

- Gambling instructional manuals and how-to-guides are the most famous products among people. These products can deliver very good results for you.

- Health products and their variations seem to sell very high on ClcikBank. Products those include drugs, supplements. Medicines, weight loss, diet plans and other similar products can help you sell in large quantities. Use these products to make more amount of money.

✍ Programs that provide bonuses and freebies are also very good.

✍ Choose products that give you a conversion ratio of 1:10 or less consistently! You give away a free survey for the contact information and get payment of around $4 to $5 for every lead very easily.

## Promote Product via Review Page

When Google made significant changes to its algorithm system and controlled the scope of Google Cash method, many affiliate marketers decided to create one-page review sites. If you type an internet marketing term like "Adwords" in all probability, you may see the word "review" in the URL.

Click on the ad and you will go to a page where the advertiser/affiliate will have a number of reviews of the top-selling products in a particular niche.

This seems to be more profitable than blind and hasty direct linking because you are adding more value to the products. Thus, you can write your own "pre-sell" copies for advocating a product and creating an honest and true review.

## Part-3
# Top 24 Tips to Maximize your Clicks

**1)** Please be extremely careful while paying more than 5 cents per click until you get a sense of the whole program. Make sure that you refine, fine tune and narrow down the search until you get a good phrase with a low rate. The downside of low cost clicks is that they have a very low conversion ratio. Once you start getting clicks to your ads, you can refine your ad and start paying better for the search terms.

2) The very few words and characters that you use in your text link ad should attract and cajole viewers to click on your ad text. Master the nuance of dynamic marketing language that will make the web site visitor to take a definite action. Also, make sure the web users land on your page after they click.

Using a page different from your homepage as your landing page may make things difficult sometimes. The main goal here is to ensure that your web site visitor will get a feeling that visiting your page is a good idea. Some users are notorious for clicking their back button of the browser so that they will make an exit you are your page before the actual conversion process. back button and you just lost the cost-per-click.

**3)** Initially, bid for low paying keywords. As you gain skill and experience and learn to confirm about fixing the maximum rate per bid. Later, you can raise your bids slowly to generate more traffic. For example, if each sale turns out a $10 profit and a given keyword needs 20 visitors to confirm a sale, then the break-even point & upper bid limit will be $.50 per click. When the bid is lower than $.50 limit, you can easily enhance your profit.

**4)** Again initially, opt for a low daily budget, like $5 that should be a great way to start your AdWords adventure. In the beginning, observe your ads very closely, change, and tweak them as and when necessary.

**5)** Create your keyword list together first, then draft and prepare your ad text. Always target key phrases, avoid using generic terms.

**6)** Use the exact keywords or phrases in the title of your ad for getting a higher CTR.

**7)** Test two ads simultaneously. Google Adwords allow you to run two different ads with your keywords so that you can compare ad performances. Keep the ad with the higher CTR and replace the other ad with a new one.

**8)** Test, tweak and adjust the Ad copy. Tweak your Ad copy to get better CTR.

**9)** Lower ad positions have a better ROI in some markets but they may not provide you adequate distribution to make better profits. Google Adwords always lists the top 1 to 3 ads above the regular search results. The top ads usually have a high click through rate that always results in lower click costs. The ad position on the Google SERP right column is fixed by the equation - max bid times ad click through rate. Before an ad can come on the top, it has to be reviewed manually and the ad should be extremely relevant.

**10)** To get a higher CTR, use exact keyword matching by placing your keyword/s in square brackets:
[buy fresh flowers]
[fresh flowers]

Your ad will not appear on the search pages for queries that include other keywords.

**11)** Ensure that you are creating negative keywords for the terms that are unconnected to your campaign. With this you can exercise more control on who sees your ads so that you will not pay for clicks that do not produce well-targeted results.

When keywords are negative-matched, your ad will not display if the web user's search includes that word. Place the negative character (-) just in front of the keyword. For example, if your keyword is flowers and your negative keyword is -free, your ad will not display when a user searches on *free flowers*.

**12)** Include both singular and plural versions of keywords so that you can have better CTR.

**13)** Add or supplement more numbers of keywords and more groups of keywords.

**14)** Create a separate Ad Group and Ads for your misspellings list, another one for your abbreviated keyword phrases, and many other variations.

**15)** Make sure that you are checking your Affiliate URL link, with Affiliate ID included in the link. Test your Adwords to make sure you end up at the desired landing page.

**16)** Evaluate your adwords after one week to make necessary changes. Google automatically disables the keywords with very low CTR. You can write Google to re launch those words again after tweaking their ad texts. Be perfect in writing better ads.

**17)** During the holiday season, you may see much activity in the internet search engines; there may be a significant increase in clicks, and better conversion rates. Many people buy during this season. Run as many Adwords running as possible during this period.

**18)** If you are a member of online forums, boards and blogs, you can include your affiliate link in the signature file. This will help you publicize your web pages and your name. Ensure People respect you and your business when you post well-written articles and blogs

**19)** Ensure that your ads inform people what you expect them to do when they enter your landing page. If you want them to buy, make sure that they do it.

**20)** Direct your people to the page that connects to your ad text. Do not, leave them guessing.

**21)** Make the sign up process simple and straight forward. Do not waste your web user's time. Always give them something of equal or greater value for the details they provide you.

**22)** Make sure that you keep up your promises of good quality and pricing.

**23)** Let your offer be filled with excitement and thrill. Be creative and entertaining when you make your offer.

**24)** Here is a very good and practical idea. Use eBay to get productive clicks and later bring visitors to your affiliate merchant sites.

The online auction site eBay.com is the 12th most visited site on the Internet, with more than 40 million members and 2 billion page views per month. This huge traffic is a clear advantage to you. Once you create an account with eBay, you can add a few numbers of affiliate links in your description.

**E**-bay has a rigid rule that prevents you from sending an eBay customer directly from your auction listing to a separate affiliate website via a direct link.

A reserve price is a tool that eBay sellers can use to stimulate bidding process on their items, while keeping the option of not selling the product if the price quoted is too low. The result is that you can get lot of exposure, and frequent commissions for a small product insertion fee of $3.30. Some of my Mobile Phone Auctions receive thousands of page views and a fraction of those follows my Mobile Phone Affiliate links and purchase from Nokia.

This approach gives a great level of income. Let us say that you will create an auction for $3.30. It has 3,000 page views over the 10-day period, 200 clicks on the links and you get two confirmed sales. All this is for only $3.30!

**Nine Tips to Manage Your Adwords Account**

**1)** Never ever, collect hundreds of keywords in an Ad Group. This will make things difficult for your efforts for optimizing offers; it is also very cumbersome to test the effectiveness of your ads.

**2)** If you have several Ad Groups in one campaign, then create a new campaign to improve the overview of the ad program.

**3)** Organize your campaigns so that one campaign contains all your successful Ad Groups. You can then set a very high daily budget for this successful campaign. You can move or transfer ads that need to be optimized into another campaign with a lower daily budget.

**4)** Use campaigns to test and check different country and language settings. Keywords in campaigns for Austria, Poland or Switzerland often cost less than Germany.

**5)** Remember that you can easily set different daily limits for different campaigns.

**6)** Your campaigns can optimize themselves automatically and in a calibrated manner. Google automatically shuts down keywords that have low click through rates (CTR). However, it they may not be the wrong keywords.

**7)** Never ever, optimize your keywords more than needed. It is just enough to optimize on the Ad Group level rather over each keyword. This is particularly effective when the keywords in an Ad Group represent the same "idea" or "theme"

**8)** "Content targeting," helps your ads appear on Google's partner sites instead of on Google search sites. Make sure that you are deactivating this from your campaign.

**9)** Some Google Adwords functions, such as geo-targeting, can be used for the Google search results pages. These functions will have no effect on Google partner sites.

**Negative Keywords**

Be serious in finding good negative words. Desist from including only positive keywords in your campaign.

Positive keywords may *bring* you traffic, while negative keywords *filter or sift* it for you, so only high quality searchers come to your ad campaign. A comprehensive list of negative keywords will increase the quality of your traffic and improve your CTR significantly.

You can also use negative keywords to display an ad for specific target groups. A flower seller might want to exclude people who are searching for books on bouquet making. The seller could enter "book" and "books" as negative keywords.

Lists of negative keywords are:

| | | |
|---|---|---|
| -affordable | -auction | -auctions |
| -bankruptcy | -bargain | -basement |
| -bargains | - counter | -cheap |
| -cheapskate | -classified ad | -classified ads |
| -coupon | -cut-rate | -deal |
| -direct sale | -dirt cheap | -discount |
| -discounter | -eBay | -economical |
| -factory outlet | -factory sale | -gently used |
| -good buy | -hand down | -inexpensive |
| -low-cost | -lowered | -low-priced |
| -low-quality | -erotic | -comparison |
| -comparison test | -comparison tests | -comparisons |
| -conference | -congress | -convention |
| -course | -courses | -DYI |

| -e book | -e books | -email |
|---|---|---|
| -essay | -event | -ezine |
| -ezines | -field report | -field reports |
| -graphic | -graphics | -agency |
| -appraiser | -consultant | -consultation |
| -consultations | -craftsman | -chargeless |
| -affiliate | - article | -customer care |
| -customer | -consultation | -article |
| -blog | -blogs | -book |
| -books | -brochure | -brochures |
| -compare | -earn | compliment |
| -costless | -exempt | -free |
| -intimate | -gift | -gratis |
| -gratuitous | -information | - material |
| -instruction | -jpeg | -jpg |
| -journal | -lust | - manual |
| -naked | -no charge | -no cost |
| -nude | -lotteries | -magazine |
| -magazines | - manuscript | -meeting |
| -mp3 | -new | -news |
| -newsletter | - newspaper | -organize |
| -photo | -photos | -picture |
| -pictures | -poem | -product |
| -raffle | -recipe | -recipes |
| -request | -requests | -review |
| -reasonable | -reduced | -repair |
| -partner | -samples | -save |

| -second-hand | -sex | -sexy |
|---|---|---|
| -seminar | -seminars | - sweepstake |
| -skimp | -special item | -stingy |
| -sale | -sample | -service |
| -services | -specialist | -text |
| -texts | -tightwad | -trial |
| -trials | -training | -test |
| -test report | -test reports | -tests |
| -un-costly | -user's manual | -used |
| -webcam | -webcams | -weblog |
| -voucher | -vouchers | -wholesale |

### Powerful Expression Keywords

| | |
|---|---|
| 10 reasons for ___! | 10 tips for ___ |
| 10 tips to ___ | 100% ___! |
| 3 ways to ___! | 7 reasons for ___ |
| About ___ offers! | Access now! |
| Access! | Act now! |
| Affordable! | All models! |
| All sizes! | All-purpose ___! |
| Alternative to ___ | Always ___! |
| And the price! | Ask us! |
| Available immediately! | Available now! |
| Bargain price! | Be the first! |
| Before it is too late! | Everything ___! |
| Everything about ___ | Everything for ___ |
| Everything in stock! | Exclusive at ___! |
| Experience it! | Fact: ___! |

| | |
|---|---|
| Falling costs! | Fast! |
| Faster than ___! | Finally ___? |
| Flexible payment! | For ___ only |
| For ___! | For every budget! |
| For lovers of ___! | For you! |
| Free catalog! | Free consultation! |
| Free delivery! | Free for ___! |
| Free for all ___! | Free offer! |
| Free shipping from _ | Free shipping! |
| Free to the door! | Free trial! |
| Hot prices! | How you ___ |
| Ideal for ___! | Immediate ___! |
| Immediate delivery! | Important for ___ |
| Including ___ | Increase ___! |
| Innovation! | Introduction price! |
| It works! | Larger than ___! |
| Last chance to ___ | Last chance! |
| Last day! | More revenue with _ |
| More success with __ | Nationwide! |
| New in ___! | New! |
| New: ___! | No minimum order |
| No obligation to buy | No problem! |
| Offer: ___! | Once in a lifetime __ |
| Only ___ days left! | Satisfaction guarantee! |
| Save also! | Step-by-step to ___! |
| Test now ___ days! | Test today! |
| That is the solution! | The ___ of the future! |

| | |
|---|---|
| The alternative! | Unlimited access! |
| Unsatisfied with ___ | Use ___! |
| We make sure that _ | We show you how! |
| While supplies last! | Why ___ |
| Why pay more? | With consultation! |
| Works every time! | You need ___? |
| You want ___? | Your chance to ___ |
| Your chance! | Yours only |

**T**ools

## The Adwords Analyzer

The Adwords Analyzer is a great and efficient tool that can help you save lot of time and identify niche markets with very little competition.

You can now enter a keyword into the Analyzer. It automatically shows you:

- A comprehensive list of all RELATED keyword phrases!

- The number of connected searches throughout the previous month for each keyword phrase!

- The number of advertising campaigns that currently exist - for both

http://www.competitioneq.com/adwords-analyzer.html

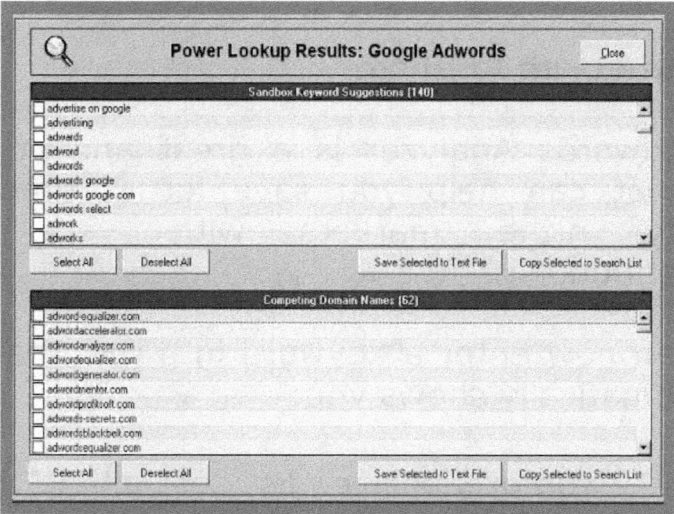

Adwords Analyzer is a good tool because it works quickly to display results that are very easy and flexible to understand. It can instantly identify underdeveloped and hidden niches, and those search terms that are worth building campaigns around.

You can save the results in a variety of ways, including as an Excel spreadsheet. It is cheap, flexible and time saving.

## Keyword Suggestion Tool

The most dangerous and negative keyword strategy is one that is too broad and non-specific. Broad keywords are usually thoughtless or useless keywords, and Google advertising always punishes lazy marketers.

The invisible danger is that you lose your hard-earned money by deploying too general keywords apart from losing your precious time. Fuzzy and false targeting may never get you the click you always wanted. In this way, you will waste your money and time because of involvement of large number of impressions before getting any meaningful CTR. Google may not like those advertisers who are not skilled enough to provide good results.

Targeted relevance is the most important and ultimate key. The more precise your targeting is the more precisely your ad's keyword matches both your ad copy and the searcher's keyword — the more magnetic your ad. The Keyword Suggestion Tool is also an efficient tool that can help you conduct research with your keywords. To find this tool:

- ☞ Click the Campaign Management tab.
- ☞ Click Tools.
- ☞ Click Keyword Suggestion Tool.

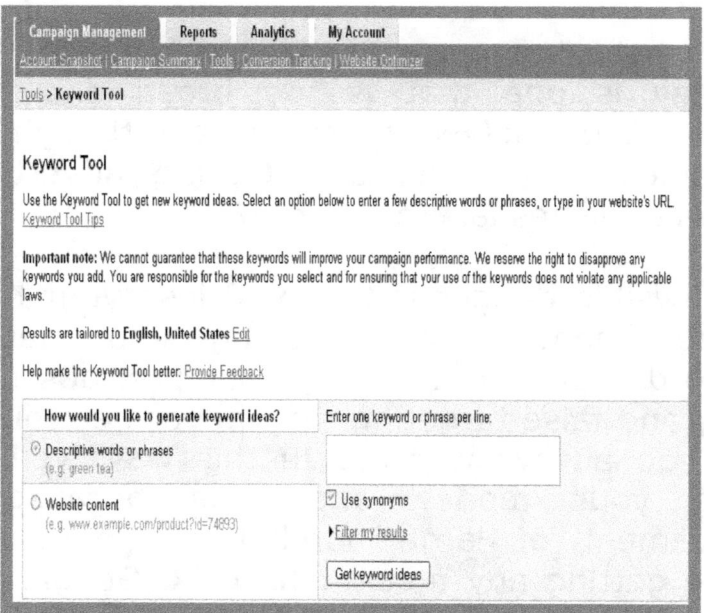

The Keyword Suggestion tool can help you spit out search terms related to one or more keywords of your choice. You can enter any combination of words to arrive at a list of most usable keyword phrases.

## Thesaurus tools

You can use an online thesaurus, in two free varieties, and they can help you find keyword variations very easily.

Log on to http://thesaurus.reference.com to read the online version of **R**oget's New Millennium Thesaurus. Type your keyword into the text box near the top of the page and click the Search Button.

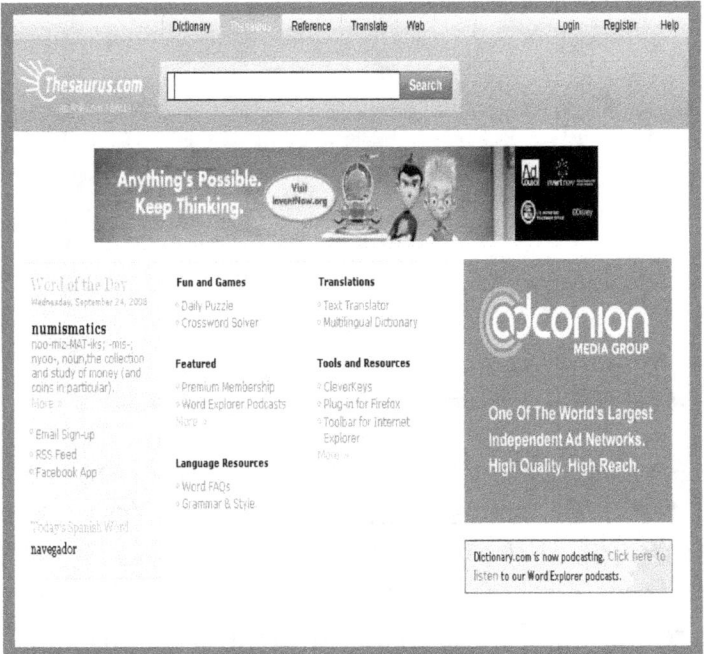

## KeyCompete.com

KeyCompete.com is one of several paid tools that come highly recommended. Log on to www.keycompete.com, type a keyword in the search box, and then click the Search button.

Now, you can get a list of Web sites bidding on that particular keyword, as shown in the following image.

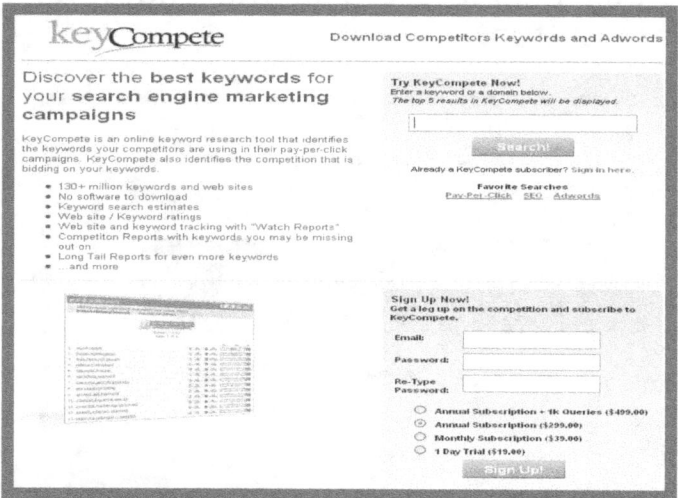

Click any of the Web site links to check a long list of their other related keywords. You can now buy individual keyword results for only $5, or purchase a single day's access to the system for a low fee of $19. An annual subscription is $299. This tool helps you compete with efficient and seasoned affiliate and Google marketers.

The Best Damn **Google Adwords** Book

Written By: Harry J. Misner

This book has been self-published & ghost written. So if you notice any grammatical errors or changes that you think should be made, please send an email to: **books@harrymisner.com**

I try to revise the book once every quarter until its perfect, and if you send me an email with proof of purchase & the recommended changes that need to be made, you'll receive the revised & updated PDF version of the book in a reply email when/if the change has been made FREE of Charge!

## "God Bless to all My Family & Friends. You are always in my prayers whether I tell you daily or not"

**Harry J. Misner**

## FREE BONUS

Once my new website is finished being designed, everyone who purchases any of my books will be granted lifetime access using the login information below:

**http://www.harrymisner.com/google**

username: customer

password: appreciation

Here you will be able to ask me any questions you might have via email and purchase updated or additional books & eBooks of mine at a discounted rate.

Dedication: I dedicate this book to my beautiful son Collin, who just turned 3 years old this September and is currently battling Autism. I constantly call him my little Angel, because he has changed my life more than I have ever dreamed or imagined possible.

I love you buddy!

"Today, 1 in 150 individuals are diagnosed with autism, making it more common than pediatric cancer, diabetes, and AIDS combined."

So please help the fight, visit
http://www.autismspeaks.org/

The Best Damn
**Google Adwords**
Book

Written By: Harry J. Misner

These next few pages are used for Book & Search Engine purposes only! The Top Google Searches for the terms: Google, Adwords, Google Adwords, Advertising, and PPC.

10.4.11 Ppc, 20 Ppc, 3. Advertising, About Advertising, Accelerator Adword, Action Advertising, Ad, Ad Agencies, Ad Agency, Ad Sense, Ad Word, Ad Words, Ad Words Select, Addwords, Ads, Ads By Google, Adsence, Adsense, Adsense Keywords, Adult Advertising, Adult Ppc, Advertise, Advertise Adwords, Advertise On Google, Advertise With Google, Advertisement, Advertisements, Advertisers, Advertising, Advertising 101, Advertising Ads, Advertising Advertisement, Advertising Advertisements, Advertising Agencies, Advertising Agency, Advertising And Marketing, Advertising Article, Advertising Awards, Advertising Billboards, Advertising Blogs, Advertising Business, Advertising Campaign, Advertising Campaigns, Advertising Clients, Advertising Commercials, Advertising Communication, Advertising Companies, Advertising Company, Advertising Concepts, Advertising Consultants, Advertising Cost, Advertising Costs, Advertising Design, Advertising Education, Advertising Effectiveness, Advertising Examples, Advertising Finance, Advertising Firms, Advertising Forum, Advertising Group, Advertising History, Advertising Images, Advertising In America, Advertising Inc, Advertising Industry, Advertising Information, Advertising Jobs, Advertising Logos, Advertising Major, Advertising Management, Advertising Market, Advertising Materials, Advertising Media, Advertising Network, Advertising On Google, Advertising On The Internet, Advertising Photos, Advertising Pictures, Advertising Prices, Advertising Pricing, Advertising Program, Advertising Promotion, Advertising Promotions, Advertising Rates, Advertising Research, Advertising Sales, Advertising Service, Advertising Services, Advertising Site, Advertising Software, Advertising Specialist, Advertising Strategies, Advertising Strategy, Advertising Techniques, Advertising Technology, Advertising Tips, Advertising Top, Advertising With Google, Advertizing, Advertsing, Adword, Adword Com, Adword Editor, Adword Google Com, Adword Login, Adword Representative, Adword Software, Adword Spy, Adwords, Adwords .com, Adwords 180, Adwords Accelerator, Adwords Account, Adwords Ads, Adwords Adsense, Adwords Advertisers, Adwords Advertising, Adwords Advice, Adwords Affiliate, Adwords Alternative, Adwords Analyzer, Adwords Api, Adwords Arbitrage, Adwords Bid, Adwords Bidding, Adwords Bids, Adwords Blog, Adwords Book, Adwords Books, Adwords Campaign, Adwords Campaign Management, Adwords Cc Google Comca, Adwords Click Fraud, Adwords Clicks, Adwords Co Uk, Adwords Com, Adwords Company, Adwords Competition, Adwords Consultant, Adwords Consultants, Adwords Contact Google, Adwords Content, Adwords Content Network, Adwords Conversion, Adwords Conversion Tracking, Adwords Cost.

The Best Damn **Google Adwords** Book

Written By: Harry J. Misner

Adwords Coupon, Adwords Coupons, Adwords Course, Adwords Cpc, Adwords Cpm, Adwords Credit, Adwords Ctr, Adwords Dominator, Adwords Editor, Adwords Editorial Guidelines, Adwords Elite, Adwords Estimator, Adwords Exam, Adwords Expert, Adwords Experts, Adwords Faq, Adwords For Beginners, Adwords For Free, Adwords Forum, Adwords Forums, Adwords Generator, Adwords Google Com, Adwords Google Make Money, Adwords Google Tip, Adwords Google Tutorial, Adwords Guide, Adwords Help, Adwords Help Center, Adwords Keyword, Adwords Keyword Insertion, Adwords Keyword Tools, Adwords Keywords, Adwords Learning, Adwords Learning Center, Adwords Local, Adwords Log, Adwords Login, Adwords Make Money, Adwords Management, Adwords Manager, Adwords Marketing, Adwords Miracle, Adwords Optimization, Adwords Pay Per Click, Adwords Phone Number, Adwords Ppc, Adwords Professional, Adwords Professionals, Adwords Promotional Code, Adwords Promotional Codes, Adwords Qualified Company, Adwords Quality Score, Adwords Ranking, Adwords Results, Adwords Revenue, Adwords Reviews, Adwords Roi, Adwords Sandbox, Adwords Search, Adwords Secret, Adwords Secrets, Adwords Select, Adwords Seminar, Adwords Seminars, Adwords Seo, Adwords Sign, Adwords Software, Adwords Specialist, Adwords Specialists, Adwords Spy, Adwords Strategy, Adwords Success, Adwords Suggestion, Adwords Suggestions, Adwords Support, Adwords Terms, Adwords Tips, Adwords Tool, Adwords Tools, Adwords Tracker, Adwords Tracking, Adwords Traffic, Adwords Traffic Estimator, Adwords Training, Adwords Tricks, Adwords Tutorial, Adwords Tutorials, Adwords Video, Adwords Voucher, Adwords Vouchers, Adwords Wrapper, Adwords.generator, Affiliate, Agency Internet Marketing, Apps, Arch Ppc, Auto Advertising, B2b Advertising, Banner Advertising, Beat Adwords, Beating Adwords, Best Advertising, Best Adwords, Best Ppc, Billboard Advertising, Billboards, Blog Advertising, Brand Advertising, Brand Management, Brand Marketing, Branding, Branding Advertising, Branding Campaign, Buy Google Adwords, Buy Ppc, Cable Advertising, Campaign, Campaigns, Click Fraud, Clickbank Adwords, Coca Cola Advertising, Commercial Advertising, Commercials, Content Adwords, Copywriting, Create Adwords, Creative Advertising, Define Advertising, Definitive Guide To Google Adwords, Design Agency, Device, Devices, Digital Marketing Agency, Direct Mail, Direct Mail Advertising, Direct Mail Marketing, Direct Marketing, Directory Advertising, Effective Advertising, Efficient Ppc, Email Marketing, Event Marketing, Exclusive Advertising, Find Advertising, Find Advertising Company, Find Advertising Services, Free Advertising, Free Adword, Free Adwords, Free Adwords Credit, Free Adwords Voucher, Free Google Ads, Free Google Adwords, Free Online Advertising, Free Pay Per Click, Free Ppc, Free Ppc Ads, Freeware, Freeware For Pocket Pc, Freeware Pocket Pc, Freewareppc, Gay Advertising, Get Rich Quick, Global Advertising.

Gmail Ppc, Good Advertising, Good Adwords, Google, Google Ad Sense, Google Ad Word, Google Ad Words, Google Ads, Google Adsense, Google Adsense Adwords, Google Advertise, Google Advertising, Google Advertising Professional, Google Adword, Google Adword Promotional Code, Google Adwords, Google Adwords 123, Google Adwords Account, Google Adwords Ads, Google Adwords Advertising, Google Adwords Affiliate, Google Adwords Alert, Google Adwords Analyzer, Google Adwords Api, Google Adwords Blog, Google Adwords Book, Google Adwords Campaign, Google Adwords Campaign Management, Google Adwords Cc, Google Adwords Certification, Google Adwords Certified, Google Adwords Class, Google Adwords Click Fraud, Google Adwords Clicks, Google Adwords Code, Google Adwords Consultant, Google Adwords Content, Google Adwords Conversion, Google Adwords Cost, Google Adwords Coupon, Google Adwords Course, Google Adwords Cpc, Google Adwords Cpm, Google Adwords Credit, Google Adwords Ctr, Google Adwords Discount, Google Adwords Editor, Google Adwords Expert, Google Adwords For Dummies, Google Adwords Forum, Google Adwords Generator, Google Adwords Guide, Google Adwords Help, Google Adwords Keyword, Google Adwords Keyword Tool, Google Adwords Keywords, Google Adwords Learning, Google Adwords Learning Center, Google Adwords Learning Centre, Google Adwords Login, Google Adwords Logo, Google Adwords Management, Google Adwords Marketing, Google Adwords Pay, Google Adwords Pay Per Click, Google Adwords Preview, Google Adwords Professional, Google Adwords Promo, Google Adwords Promo Code, Google Adwords Promotion, Google Adwords Promotion Code, Google Adwords Promotional, Google Adwords Promotional Code, Google Adwords Promotional Codes, Google Adwords Report, Google Adwords Results, Google Adwords Revenue, Google Adwords Review, Google Adwords Scam, Google Adwords Secrets, Google Adwords Select, Google Adwords Seminar, Google Adwords Seminars, Google Adwords Software, Google Adwords Specialist, Google Adwords Suggestions, Google Adwords Support, Google Adwords Team, Google Adwords Terms, Google Adwords Tips, Google Adwords Tool, Google Adwords Tools, Google Adwords Tracker, Google Adwords Tracking, Google Adwords Traffic, Google Adwords Training, Google Adwords Tricks, Google Adwords Video, Google Adwords Voucher, Google Cash, Google Keyword, Google Ltd Adwords, Google Make Money, Google Ppc, Google Sandbox, Google Search Adwords, Google Search Engine, Google's Adwords, Googleadword, Googlecash, Googles Adwords, Gps, Great Advertising, Green Advertising, Guide To Google Adwords, Handheld Pc, Healthcare Advertising, How To Use Google Adwords, Http Adwords Google Com, I-mate, Image Advertising, Imate, Inside Adwords, Interactive Advertising, Internet Advertising, Internet Advertising Company, Internet Marketing, Internet Money, Ipaq, Iso Ppc, Jay Advertising, Jobs From Home.

Keyword Suggestion Tool, Keywords, Lawless Ppc, Learn Adwords, Learning Google Adwords, Legal Advertising, Local Advertising, Local Online Advertising, Local/ Ppc, Low Cost Advertising, Magazine Advertising, Mail Advertising, Make Money, Make Money With Google Adwords, Manage Adwords, Manage Ppc, Marketing, Marketing Advertising, Marketing Agencies, Marketing Agency, Marketing Campaign, Marketing Campaigns, Marketing Communications, Marketing Company, Marketing Consultants, Marketing Management, Marketing Research, Marketing Strategies, Marketing Strategy, May Advertising, Mobile 2003, Mobile Advertising, Mobile Marketing, Most Expensive Adwords, Mother Advertising, Msn Adwords, National Advertising, New Ppc, Newspaper Advertising, No Investment, Online Ads, Online Advertising, Online Advertising Company, Online Advertising Network, Online Advertising Services, Online Marketing, Online Marketing Agency, Online Web Site Advertising, Orange Ppc, Outdoor Advertising, Overture, Overture Adwords, Overture Keyword, Overture Keyword Tool, Overture Suggestion Tool, Palm Os, Palm Ppc, Pay Per Click, Pay Per Click Advertising, Pay Per Click Companies, Pay Per Click Google, Pda, Pda Software, Pda Themes, Perry, Perry Adwords, Perry Marshall Google Adwords, Platform Advertising, Pocket, Pocket Informant, Pocket Pc, Pocket Pc 2003, Pocket Pc Applications, Pocket Pc Download, Pocket Pc Downloads, Pocket Pc Free Themes, Pocket Pc Games, Pocket Pc Software, Pocket Pc Theme, Pocket Pcs, Pocket Ppc, Pocket Streets, Pocket Themes, Pocketgear, Pocketpc, Pocketpc Software, Pocketpccity, Ppc, Ppc 1, Ppc 100, Ppc 2000, Ppc 2002, Ppc 440, Ppc 6700, Ppc 6900, Ppc 7000, Ppc 750, Ppc Account, Ppc Ad, Ppc Advertisement, Ppc Advertiser, Ppc Advertising, Ppc Agency, Ppc App, Ppc Applications, Ppc Apps, Ppc Arm, Ppc Battery, Ppc Blog, Ppc Bluetooth, Ppc Browser, Ppc Buildos, Ppc Calculator, Ppc Campaign, Ppc Campaign Management, Ppc Chess, Ppc Com, Ppc Companies, Ppc Company, Ppc Competition, Ppc Compression, Ppc Computer, Ppc Consultant, Ppc Consulting, Ppc Contact, Ppc Cost, Ppc Course, Ppc Design, Ppc Desktop, Ppc Download, Ppc E Tools, Ppc Email, Ppc Emulator, Ppc Expert, Ppc Experts, Ppc Flying, Ppc Forms, Ppc Formula, Ppc Forum, Ppc Forums, Ppc Freeware, Ppc Geeks, Ppc Gps, Ppc Guide, Ppc Handheld, Ppc Help, Ppc Hero, Ppc Home, Ppc Industries, Ppc International, Ppc Ipaq, Ppc Keyboard, Ppc Landscape, Ppc Live, Ppc Login, Ppc Management, Ppc Management Software, Ppc Manager, Ppc Managment, Ppc Marketing, Ppc Music, Ppc Network, Ppc Online, Ppc Online Com, Ppc Os, Ppc Pda, Ppc Player, Ppc Program, Ppc Programs, Ppc Quote, Ppc Remote, Ppc Research, Ppc Reviews, Ppc Search, Ppc Service, Ppc Services, Ppc Shareware, Ppc Sites, Ppc Skins, Ppc Smartphone, Ppc Soft, Ppc Software, Ppc Solution, Ppc Specialist, Ppc Support, Ppc Sync, Ppc Tech, Ppc Theme, Ppc Themes, Ppc Thompson, Ppc Thompson Com, Ppc Tips, Ppc Today, Ppc Tools, Ppc Touch, Ppc Training, Ppc Tutorial, Ppc Uk.

The Best Damn
**Google Adwords**
Book
Written By: Harry J. Misner

Ppc Version, Ppc Video, Ppc Warez, Ppc Website, Ppc Wifi, Ppc Wiki, Ppc Worldwide, Print Advertising, Product Advertising, Profit From Google Adwords, Promotion, Promotional, Promotional Advertising, Promotions, Public Relations, Publicity, Radio Advertising, Retail Advertising, Sales, Search Engine Advertising, Search Term Suggestion Tool, Sem Ppc, Seo, Services Marketing, Sh3, Shareware, Silverlight Ppc, Small Business Advertising, Smartphone, Software, Software For Pocket Pc, Speed Ppc, Strategic Marketing, Street Advertising, Subliminal Advertising, Suggestion Tool, Targeted Advertising, Television Advertising, The Definitive Guide To Google Adwords, Themes Pocket Pc, Top Advertising Agencies, Top Ppc, Tv Advertising, Using Adwords, Using Google Adwords, Vga Ppc, Vision Advertising, Wade Winger, Web Advertising, Web Marketing, Web Site Advertising, Web Site Internet Advertising, Website Advertising, Website Promotion, West Advertising, Wince, Wince Ppc, Windows Ce, Windows Mobile, Windows Mobile 2003, Windows Mobile Ppc, Windowsce, Winning Results With Google Adwords, Wm2003, Write Google Adwords, Writing Adwords, Www Adword Google Com, Www Google Adwords Com, Www.google-adwords, Xda, Xda Ppc, Xscale, Youtube Advertising, Youtube On Ppc, Youtube Ppc.

## The common misspellings for the terms: oogle, Adwords, Google Adwords, Advertising, and PPC.

Google, Oogle, Gogle, Goole, Googe, Googl, Ogogle, Gogole, Goolge, Googel, Ggoogle, Gooogle, Googgle, Googlle, Googlee, Foogle, Hoogle, Giogle, Gpogle, Goigle, Gopgle, Goofle, Goohle, Googke, Goog;e, Googlw, Googlr, Toogle, Yoogle, Boogle, Voogle, G9ogle, G0ogle, Glogle, Gkogle, Go9gle, Go0gle, Golgle, Gokgle, Gootle, Gooyle, Gooble, Goovle, Googoe, Googpe, Goog.e, Goog,e, Googl3, Googl4, Googld, Googls, Google Adwords, Googleadwords, Adwords Google, Oogle Adwords, Gogle Adwords, Goole Adwords, Googe Adwords, Googl Adwords, Google Dwords, Google Awords, Google Adords, Google Adwrds, Google Adwods, Google Adwors, Google Adword, Ogogle Adwords, Gogole Adwords, Goolge Adwords, Googel Adwords, Google Dawords, Google Awdords, Google Adowrds, Google Adwrods, Google Adwodrs, Google Adworsd, Ggoogle Adwords, Gooogle Adwords, Googgle Adwords, Googlle Adwords, Googlee Adwords, Google Aadwords, Google Addwords, Google Adwwords, Google Adwoords, Google Adworrds, Google Adwordds, Google Adwordss, Foogle Adwords, Hoogle Adwords, Giogle Adwords, Gpogle Adwords, Goigle Adwords, Gopgle Adwords, Goofle Adwords, Goohle Adwords, Googke Adwords, Goog;e Adwords, Googlw Adwords, Googlr Adwords, Google Sdwords, Google Aswords, Google Afwords, Google Adqords, Google Adeords, Google Adwirds, Google Adwprds, Google Adwoeds, Google Adwotds, Google Adworss, Google Adworfs, Google Adworda, Google Adwordd, Toogle Adwords.

Yoogle Adwords, Boogle Adwords, Voogle Adwords, G9ogle Adwords, G0ogle Adwords, Glogle Adwords, Gkogle Adwords, Go9gle Adwords, Go0gle Adwords, Golgle Adwords, Gokgle Adwords, Gootle Adwords, Gooyle Adwords, Gooble Adwords, Goovle Adwords, Googoe Adwords, Googpe Adwords, Goog.e Adwords, Goog,e Adwords, Googl3 Adwords, Googl4 Adwords, Googld Adwords, Googls Adwords, Google Qdwords, Google Wdwords, Google Zdwords, Google Aewords, Google Arwords, Google Acwords, Google Axwords, Google Ad2ords, Google Ad3ords, Google Adsords, Google Adaords, Google Adw9rds, Google Adw0rds, Google Adwlrds, Google Adwkrds, Google Adwo4ds, Google Adwo5ds, Google Adwofds, Google Adwodds, Google Adwores, Google Adworrs, Google Adworcs, Google Adworxs, Google Adwordw, Google Adworde, Google Adwordx, Google Adwordz, Adwords, Dwords, Awords, Adords, Adwrds, Adwods, Adwors, Adword, Dawords, Awdords, Adowrds, Adwrods, Adwodrs, Adworsd, Aadwords, Addwords, Adwwords, Adwoords, Adworrds, Adwordds, Adwordss, Sdwords, Aswords, Afwords, Adqords, Adeords, Adwirds, Adwprds, Adwoeds, Adwotds, Adworss, Adworfs, Adworda, Adwordd, Qdwords, Wdwords, Zdwords, Aewords, Arwords, Acwords, Axwords, Ad2ords, Ad3ords, Adsords, Adaords, Adw9rds, Adw0rds, Adwlrds, Adwkrds, Adwo4ds, Adwo5ds, Adwofds, Adwodds, Adwores, Adworrs, Adworcs, Adworxs, Adwordw, Adworde, Adwordx, Adwordz, Advertising, Dvertising, Avertising, Adertising, Advrtising, Advetising, Adverising, Advertsing, Advertiing, Advertisng, Advertisig, Advertisin, Davertising, Avdertising, Adevrtising, Advretising, Advetrising, Adveritsing, Advertsiing, Advertiisng, Advertisnig, Advertisign, Aadvertising, Addvertising, Advvertising, Adveertising, Adverrtising, Adverttising, Advertiising, Advertissing, Advertisiing, Advertisinng, Advertisingg, Sdvertising, Asvertising, Afvertising, Adcertising, Adbertising, Advwrtising, Advrrtising, Adveetising, Advettising, Adverrising, Adveryising, Advertusing, Advertosing, Advertiaing, Advertiding, Advertisung, Advertisong, Advertisibg, Advertisimg, Advertisinf, Advertisinh, Qdvertising, Wdvertising, Zdvertising, Aevertising, Arvertising, Acvertising, Axvertising, Adfertising, Adgertising, Adv3rtising, Adv4rtising, Advdrtising, Advsrtising, Adve4tising, Adve5tising, Adveftising, Advedtising, Adver5ising, Adver6ising, Advergising, Adverfising, Advert8sing, Advert9sing, Advertksing, Advertjsing, Advertiwing, Advertieing, Advertixing, Advertizing, Advertis8ng, Advertis9ng, Advertiskng, Advertisjng, Advertisihg, Advertisijg, Advertisint, Advertisiny, Advertisinb, Advertisinv, Ppc, Pc, Pp, Pcp, Pppc, Ppcc, Ppx, Ppv, Ppd, Ppf.

☐ Advertising

☐ Business & Economics

☐ Business / Economics / Finance

☐ Business/Economics

☐ Advertising & Promotion

☐ Business & Economics / Advertising & Promotion

☐ Internet advertising

☐ Web search engines

☐ Sales & Marketing

Books > Computers & Internet > Business & Culture > Web Marketing
Books > Business & Investing > Industries & Professions > E-commerce
Books > Computers & Internet > Home Computing > Internet

☐ Internet

☐ Marketing

☐ Business & Economics

☐ Computer - Internet

☐ Business/Economics

☐ Computers / Internet / General

☐ Internet - General

☐ Marketing - General

☐ Software Development & Engineering - General

☐ Google AdWords

☐ Internet marketing

☐ Computing: Professional & Programming